DADMIN

A (sort of) guide to being a Dad

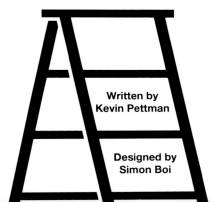

Written by
Kevin Pettman

Designed by
Simon Boi

Dadmin
Noun: (Dad - Admin) -

*The jobs Dads do
before they can relax.*

Example usage

*"I'll be out soon,
just doing some Dadmin"*

#contents

#welcometodadmin

Fixing, sorting, lifting, building, drilling, painting, mending. These words, and stacks more, are all connected with the wonderfully weird world of Dadmin. The list of jobs, tasks, missions and deeds that Dads carry out day in and day out fall neatly under this catch-all phrase. Whether you're a young Dad, new Dad, middle-aged Dad or even a Granddad, Dadmin is everywhere. Dadmin is your life. You = Dadmin. You get the message, yeah?

Welcome to
DADMIN®

Luckily, Dads actually enjoy a spot of Dadmin. They secretly revel in ticking things off from their list of Dadmin duties. This may be a quick quest to replace the TV remote batteries or a more complex crusade such as taking rubbish to the dump, putting up a shelf or unblocking drains. Of course, women are perfectly capable of carrying out such pursuits, and usually with much less palaver for the family. But for some unknown reason, it just feels right that Dad should be the one to remove spiders from the kids' bedrooms and build flat pack without following the instructions.

Dadmin: a (sort of) guide to being a Dad is the ultimate help book to steer you through this strange phenomenon of fatherhood. It's like a Dad's dossier of Dos and Don'ts, with many Dadmin details that you'll doff your cap to along the way.

Let's do some Dadmin...

CHECKLIST

 Do... read this book very carefully. Mark notes in the margins if you like.

 Don't... write rude words or pictures in the margins. You're not at school now.

#lifebeforedadmin

You don't need a fancy book – or even this trivial book, for that matter – to tell you that before the arrival of Dadmin, life was very different. Take a moment to cast your mind back to that place. It was just you, or you and your partner, and watching TV uninterrupted for six hours straight was the norm. At the weekend you could wake up whenever you liked, do whatever you liked and go wherever you liked. Things were quieter, calmer and simpler in that place. Remember it? Now that you're a Dad, please bin those memories. Accept they're lost down the back of the sofa. A sofa very much like the one you used to relax on of an evening and weekend.

Once upon a time you could take leisurely walks with the dog, waste an afternoon in Currys looking at the latest laptops and enjoy shopping trips into town with a spot of lunch.

**FAVE THINGS
TO DO BEFORE
DADMIN ARRIVED...**

- Chill out in the spare room, which is now a bedroom.

- Enjoy not knowing where the kids' channels are on Sky.

- Go to the match and not feel guilty.

- Play golf and not feel guilty.

- Do nothing. All day. Lovely.

Bloke thinking about what he could do with his day that contains no Dadmin. What is Dadmin? He is blisfully unaware at this stage.

As a Dad, 'once upon a time' is now your cue for bedtime reading, you only go to Currys if the family tumble dryer dies and eating out in town is an expensive multi-person drama you can do without, thanks.

But there's no point in doing the whole before and after thing. Play with the hand you've been dealt and tackle your Dadmin demons head on. Ask yourself this: if you don't mow the lawn, tidy the shed and Polyfilla the skirting today, who else will? Well, there is that handyman bloke who stuck a leaflet through the door recently, but not at thirty quid an hour.

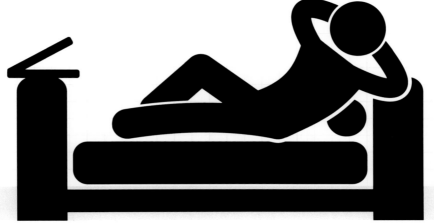

What type of Dadmin Dad are you?

Take your pick and discover your Dadmin status.

The WiFi is down and your kids need it for homework and/or tablet viewing. **Do you…?**

A: Spring into action and spend two hours talking to your internet provider to fix it.

B: While drinking your tea, turn the router off and on. And off and on again. And off…

C: Tell the children to manage without it for now, and that in your day the internet wasn't even a thing.

The family car needs cleaning. **Do you…?**

A: Wash and shampoo it with more love and attention than you do with your own body.

B: Happily give it a quick once-over, returning the vehicle to its original colour.

C: Clean the windscreen, windows and lights - in other words, the important bits.

Mostly As

You're a… Dadmin devotee
No task is too big or too little for you. You deal with Dadmin like a proper legend.
We salute you.

Mostly Bs

You're a… Dadmin doer
You're well up for dabbling in Dadmin, but need a bit of a run-up. And a cup of tea.

Mostly Cs

You're a… Dadmin dope.
Dadmin doesn't come easily to you. But, not to worry because your heart's in it, even if your hands and brain struggle.

The bathroom toilet's not flushing properly.
Do you…?

A: Dash for your toolbox and instantly get to grips with your ballcock, so to speak.

B: Watch some bloke on YouTube fix his toilet, then an hour later, realise you've just been watching YouTube videos.
And not ones about broken toilets.

C: Think about fixing it, then think you

Stuff needs to go in the loft.
Do you…?

A: Drop the loft ladder, climb it and place boxes with military precision.

B: Have a cuppa to warm yourself up first, coz it's cold up there.

C: Eventually get into the loft after you've found that stick thing that opens the hatch.

Baby Dadmin

Here we go.

Naturally, all Dadmin starts with Baby Dadmin.
But then there's Pre-Baby Dadmin before
that, like constructing the cot and painting
the nursery, before the real onslaught begins
after little'un arrives.

Just be prepared.
Or if you can, be pre-prepared.

#pushthepushchair

There's nothing more iconic, nothing that says more to the world that 'I am a Dad with a baby', than a Dad swiftly moving his baby along in a pushchair for the very first time. It's a proud moment for Dad. He's been on a great journey to get to this point... not the pregnancy and birth and all of that stuff, but selecting, buying and working out how to operate the pushchair.

Dads can spend weeks choosing a pushchair. The number of wheels, size and functions all come into play, but really he just wants to look cool pushing it. Even if his wife points out that it's heavier and less manoeuvrable than a bin lorry, he still prefers it because it's the colour of his football team and has a cup holder.

For the first few weeks, Dad treats the pushchair with incredible care. It's lovingly folded and laid into the car, the wheels wiped after every use and it has its own storage spot inside the house. That soon becomes tedious and the pushchair will be thrown into the boot like a pair of his old footy boots, the wheels will be a permo-muddy brown and will live in the garage.

CHECKLIST

 Do... load it up and treat it like a personalized shopping trolley on trips to Tesco.

 Don't... resent that the pushchair cost more than your car.

#changethenappy

Compare changing a nappy to the first time you drank beer. It was a bit horrid at first, but you soon got used to it and grew to handle it. No problem. Not that changing a stinky nappy is as fun for Dad as a cheeky Friday pint, however both are a necessity in their own way.

The sight and smell (of a dirty nappy, not beer) becomes second nature to you. At first, Dads try to accomplish the mission with their eyes closed and nose turned away, but quickly realise this is a poor technique if you want to keep the living room carpet its original colour.

The trick is to have all your essential tools at close quarters. You'll find a comprehensive list on the right. It's a good idea to keep your wife at close quarters too, just in case it changes from a one-man job into a one man and one woman operation.

CHECKLIST

- ☑ *Clean nappy*
- ☑ *Changing mat*
- ☑ *Wipes*
- ☑ *Powder*
- ☑ *Cream*
- ☑ *Cotton wool*
- ☑ *Warm water*
- ☑ *Waste bag*
- ☑ *Towel*
- ☑ *Distraction toy*
- ☑ *Clean baby vest*
- ☑ *Clean t-shirt for Dad*

#feedthebaby

It makes sense for the baby-feeding page to be opposite the nappy changing page. The two go hand in hand, so to speak – you feed your little ray of sunshine with one hand and deal with the outcome with the other.

Bottle feeding can be enjoyable for Dad and his baby. Settle in comfortably on the sofa, prop your arm up sufficiently and let him or her chug away contentedly. Dad will either gaze dotingly at his bundle of joy or, more likely, will desperately flick through the Sky box to catch up on some essential viewing. Quite how he manages to do this with one hand holding baby and the second holding the bottle, no one really knows. He just does. While sat down, Dads become multi-tasking masters.

Feeding Tips

- Do your share of nighttime bottle feeds.

- Don't fall asleep in the nursery after a nighttime bottle feed.

#dothebathtime

Get the bathtime routine right and it should be an incredibly relaxing and rewarding half hour for Dad and baby. Get it wrong and it could be a wet and miserable 30 minutes for both parties.

Experts (i.e. not you) know that evening baths can help a small child prepare for bed. It sends a calming signal to him or her that the day is drawing to a close. Bathtime, and the soon-to-follow sleeptime, also means that Dad is within touching distance of peace and quiet in the house. He'll have time to finally finish other vital Baby Dadmin duties – tidying toys, washing up orange plastic spoons and scraping baked bean juice off the cat.

CHECKLIST

 Do... load up the bath with fun toys.

 Don't... play with the toys yourself and ignore your child.

Bubbles. Lovely, lovely, bubbles.
How are bubbles formed in the bath?
Where do they disappear to?
Note: don't spend all evening looking
at the bubbles.

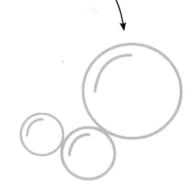

In the bathroom, the first important job is testing the water temperature. This should be around 37°C and obviously not too hot or cold for your baby. You can buy a handy temperature gauge device that floats in the water, but it's much more fun to turn yourself into some kind of laboratory assistant and constantly check and monitor the water as the bath is running. This will involve dipping your elbow or wrist in and adopting a bendy pose not out of place in a yoga class. Once you've conducted your final scientific tests of water swirling and bubble distribution, it's splashtime for baby. It's time, too, for you to painfully crouch on your knees beside the bath and prepare for the pain when you stand up again in 20 minutes.

Top bath tips

- Bathing the baby can be a great way to bond with them, and leave your partner clearing up the rest of the house.

- Try turning the water purple by mixing red and blue bubble bath.

- Don't use a jumbo car cleaning sponge to save time.

#dothepeekaboo

In any other situation, rolling around on the carpet, jumping out from behind sofas and pulling stupid faces would draw worrying looks from bystanders. But in the act of entertaining and playing with a baby, it's to be expected and indeed encouraged. Dad must have no inhibitions when it comes to playtime, even if his go-to stupid face makes him look like Shrek's uglier brother.

Playtime is a fun time for your baby and you. After all, you can't really mess about with that cool Mothercare toy truck all by yourself, so why not involve the child too? And you're desperate to devise and build an epic wooden train track that runs from the hallway to the backdoor. Don't worry if your baby can only just sit upright and won't be able to join in the fun for a good few months. You're just giving it all a good test, ready for him or her.

Whether it's bouncing baby on your knee or clapping and dancing like a crazy clown, you have no choice but to give playtime everything you've got. When else will you get to stick your tongue out and sing horribly just four centimetres away from another human's face?

CHECKLIST

 Do... *arrange cushions on the floor during playtime, for baby's and Dad's comfort.*

 Don't... *persist with playing peekaboo if the kid looks totally unimpressed.*

#givethecuddles

Ahh. Can anyone give your baby a soothing, comforting cuddle, and put a smile on his or her face quite like you can? Well, apart from your mum, wife, brother and Sue next door, no-one can.

Cuddling is the easiest Baby Dadmin on the list. It requires no tools or equipment – just thrust your arms and hands forward, pick up your child and rock, sway and snuggle away until your child is content. Or until your cuddles don't actually stop baby from crying, at which point you knock on Sue's door. Again.

CHECKLIST

 Do... give the cuddles in a quiet place, but that doesn't mean a trip to the library each time.

 Don't... say "come here and have a cuddle, wuddle, duddle with Daddy."

The science bit

- Clever people have found that cuddling and having lots of contact with your newborn baby may help influence their gene expression. It may also influence Dad's jeans if the baby decides to be sick at any point.

#putbabytosleep

Pay attention, Dads. This one is vital for the wellbeing of your baby, your partner, you, your family, neighbours, friends and workmates. Get the sleeping thing wrong and EVERYONE will suffer.

Now think back to your school days. In between you messing about with the Bunsen burners and putting Monster Munch under a microscope, the science teacher taught you about Newton's third law. In summary, this states that every action has an equal and opposite reaction. Let's apply this famous principle to your baby's sleeping needs. The action of him or her not having a mid-morning nap creates an equal and opposite reaction of constant crying and pulling out of hair. And as the baby hardly has a whisker on its head, we must assume that this refers to you pulling out your barnet, as the sleep-deprived child gets crankier each minute.

CHECKLIST

☑ Do... *follow your wife's strict sleeping schedule and routine when you're left solely in charge of the baby.*

☒ Don't... *forget that there's a strict sleeping schedule and routine when you're left solely in charge of the baby.*

If you get bored of nursery rhymes, any musical hummings will work. Maybe not a Slipknot song, though.

There are the tried and trusted techniques of singing, rocking and shushing a baby to sleep, as well as plonking them in front of CBeebies with the hope that Mr Tumble works his magic.

But not to worry because, thankfully, Dad can always take his child for a walk in the pushchair and hope that the ride gently sends the baby off to sleep. If that doesn't work, at least the screams from baby will be drowned out by the sounds of barking dogs and lorry drivers swearing at cyclists. So, every cloud…

Baby sleep tips

- It goes without saying, but don't undertake noisy Dadmin jobs such as vacuuming and drilling when the child's sleeping during the day. This time is for silent chores like knitting a jumper, flower arranging and doing a Sudoku.

#getsomesleep 😴

Dads of newborn babies will not get a decent sleep for six months.

Nights Dad gets under 5 hours sleep
(first year)

Very tired Dad, demonstrating the 'close to tears through lack of sleep' pose.

Deal with it.

Toddler Dadmin

Buckle up for the ride.

Congratulations, Dad! You've survived Baby Dadmin and you're ready to take on Toddler Dadmin.

But don't get too excited. You're escaping a time when your baby constantly made mess and noise, just to enter another period of mess and noise, with the added bonus of your kid being very mobile and now able to say no to you a lot. Fun times ahead!

#chasethetoddler

Yep, Dads do an awful lot of toddler chasing. The moment a two-year-old gets his running legs on, there's just no stopping them from going anywhere they like. Parents spend so long waiting and wishing for their lad or lassie to begin walking, only to realise it was much easier when they just parked themself on their buttski all day. A spot of casual crawling is nothing now that your child has entered into full-on running-away-from-dad-with-a-big-grin mode.

Dad has to quickly work out his toddler's range. How far can the nipper toddle away from him without causing concern? Clearly, the further the kid moves, the more ground Dad has to cover in a split second when he deems the distance between them too great.

The only solution is to rein your child in, literally. There are all sorts of straps and harnesses out there, designed to tether a roving toddler to an adult in a way that makes your little one look like an excited spaniel and you a less-than-enamoured pet owner.

CHECKLIST

 Do... invest in some new trainers. Comfy running gear is a must.

 Don't...think about taking the annoying stair gates down for at least three years.

#pottytraining

Having suffered and survived two or three years of nappy changing, facing the prospect of potty training should be a breath of fresh air. Not that your toddler using a potty usually makes the air around you very fresh, but you get the message.

The big decision is when to start the potty training process. Asking your child to sit on a lump of moulded plastic in the middle of the kitchen, while you cajole them into having a wee or a poo doesn't sound very appealing to either party. It sounds even worse if nanny, granddad, uncles, aunties and siblings are also watching on with eager anticipation. No-one likes to go in front of a crowd, do they? A wise Dad will want the whole operation done and dusted before he even thinks about changing the living room carpets.

CHECKLIST

 Do... be very patient and understanding.

Don't... think just because you housetrained the puppy in two weeks, potty training a toddler takes five days, tops.

No Dads — you can't train a three--year-old to empty their own potty into the toilet. That's your dirty job.

Even wiser Dads will wait until spring or summer time to begin the toilet turmoil, allowing his kid to run around the garden, while Dad hurls the potty under them if they stand still for a nanosecond and pull a funny face.

A potty is only about the size of a washing-up bowl (please don't confuse the two) but it will become the most dominant object in your house. Don't go thinking it can be hidden away under the stairs and only whipped out when called upon. Oh no. The potty must be kept on display at all times so that junior becomes familiar with it and harbours no ill feeling towards its presence. After a few weeks your kid will have it mastered and the thought of not having to clean the floor every 30 minutes won't seem so potty.

Potty training tips

- Always keep one potty upstairs and another downstairs. Constantly running up and down the stairs will help improve your cardio but not the state of your carpets.

#feedthetoddler

Whereas anything goes when feeding older kids – for example, mixing spaghetti hoops with Hula Hoops won't raise an eyebrow – Dads must take a little more catering care with toddlers. There's usually an agreed system between the parents that the kids will eat a version of what they are having for lunch or dinner, albeit in a more mashed-up style. This saves money and is much quicker than faffing with separate mealtime menus for the nippers. It's also music to Dad's ears, as chicken korma and toad-in-the-hole can easily be cut, crushed or scrunched into a bright orange bowl and served at the right temperature for a toddler.

Whetting Dad's appetite further, he can really go to town on the dessert front. Kids love strawberries and ice cream, banana and rice pudding, chocolate sponge and fruit yoghurts. Much like the spaghetti and crisp combo already mentioned, you can even mix up these ingredients to create the ultimate dreamy dessert dish. Just have a stack of wet wipes nearby.

CHECKLIST

Do... use raisins as a snack. They keep kids busy for hours as they constantly drop and pick them up.

Don't... think that 3.30pm is too early to dish up dinner. Better a happy toddler than a hangry toddler.

Here comes the aeroplane. Weeeeeeeeeee!

#tellthestories

Once upon a time... Dad read a fun night-time story to his little son or daughter as they sat together on the bed. It's such a sweet and special time, as they share precious moments, bonding over creative language and pictures. The fact that Dad and his offspring have read the same story every night for the last 17 weeks, to the point where he can recite it blindfolded page by page, shouldn't be of concern.

Unfortunately though, due to the child's in-depth knowledge of the story, Dad can't employ his No1 bedtime story trick of skipping whole sentences, even pages, to finish the book quicker. If he does, his kid will pull him up proper sharpish and insist on reading it all again, doing all the funny voices and actions along the way.

Dads, it's best just to do as you're told if you want to live happily ever after.

CHECKLIST

☑ *Do... explain that The Gruffalo isn't real and can't be seen at the zoo.*

☒ *Don't... get stuck on the big words.*

---

5 fatherly bedtime reads

1. The Gruffalo
2. The Gruffalo's Child
3. That Roald Dahl book you once read at school
4. 2010 World Cup Panini sticker album
5. Some other book by Julia Donaldson

#packthecar

Every Dad knows that even a simple car journey to the shops turns into a tumultuous trek when there's a toddler in tow. While these trips are not quite as traumatic as they were in the baby stage, as there's no need for postman-size nappy changing bags and three crates of toys and bottles, there's still an endless catalogue of stuff to shove in the car. And that's just for short journeys – packing for holidays or an overnight stay requires Dad to be incredibly organised as he loads up the family wagon.

Whether Dad drives a fun-size Fiesta or a hulking Hummer, he'll always end up short of space. The process begins in an orderly and humane enough fashion. The pushchair slides into the boot nice and neatly, and Dad is convinced that this Dadmin task will be finished soon enough.

CHECKLIST

 Do...use every inch of space that you can find.

 Don't... forget to leave room for the kids to sit.

Annoyingly, even though your child is nearly four now, he or she may still occasionally might sort of want to maybe ride in the buggy a bit, for a while, on days out.

So, this means the pushchair remains a must on the long list of items required to pack. Stacked around it in the boot will also be things like suitcases, random bags, coats, shoes, scooters, food, drinks and just the one crate of toys. But, just as it all squeezes in the boot and inside the car and the doors can be wedged shut with enough force, Dad realises there are four rucksacks still to find room for. There's only one solution… the roof box!

Having a roof box strapped to the car is the ultimate sign of a Family On Tour. They are simply horrible and ugly contraptions. Any Dad that says having such a big piece of plastic up there actually suits his car is a big, big liar.

#chargethedevices

There's no point harking back to the time when, as a little kid, you happily played with Lego and Action Man figures from morning until night. In those days, the only personal screen time you had was kids' TV on a Saturday morning or cartoons for ten minutes after school. Nowadays, even toddlers have an array of screens, tablets and computers at their fingertips and all of them require constant charging. Luckily, Dad's an expert in this field.

For some people, sorting out which charger, plug or chord goes with which device is a total head scratcher. Not for Dad. He can sort it with his eyes closed and insert cables to computers in the blink of an eye. Come to think of it, that's actually impossible to do with your eyes closed. Proof that Dadmin transcends into the supernatural.

CHECKLIST

 Do... work out how much charge a tablet needs for a two-hour car journey.

 Don't... work out how much all this charging adds to your electricity bill.

Top tech that Dads charge

1. iPad
2. VTech laptop
3. Kids' digital camera
4. Dad's old iPhone that the kids now have
5. Dad's new iPhone that the kids also have

#taketotheparty

When kids are still babies, parties and special events clearly mean nothing to them. For them, there's no difference between Christmas, the second Thursday in April and their first birthday. But when they become toddlers, these occasions take on much significance and demand a party that even the Kardashians would be happy to attend.

The most pressured event is your own child's birthday party. Parents must deliver on multiple fronts – venue, entertainment, food, cake, food and cake allergies, the weather and finally the all-important party bags. A year is barely enough time to recover and prepare for the next annual celebration.

However, if it's not your own kid's party, turning up to these events is usually quite enjoyable and worth splashing out a fiver on a present. In return, your child is fed and entertained for a few hours and, hopefully, you should get a nice cup of tea and a sit down inside a village hall or the local play centre. If there just happens to be free WiFi, you're quids in.

CHECKLIST

 Do... remember to ask if it's okay to drop your toddler off and return and collect when it's finished.

 Don't... forget to pick your kid up again.

#teachhowtorideabike

Teaching your toddler how to pedal down the street can be tough work and put a strain on your latissimus dorsi, thoracolumbar fascia and sacrospinalis. In other words, it's back-breaking stuff. If there was an Olympic medal for leaning down to two feet, running sideways and holding a saddle at the same time, Dads would have more bling hanging from their necks than Usain Bolt.

Cycling with stabilisers on the bike is all well and good, but it's not the real deal and gives your child a false sense of security. As harsh as it may seem, they need to be exposed to the full effect of having to balance, pedal and brake all in the straight section of the cycle path at the park. The park's a great place to begin the tutoring. It's best to begin by riding over grass, as there's sure to be the odd moment of falling down (by Dad and child) which will require a soft landing. Usually in dog poo.

CHECKLIST

 Do... prepare to shed a tear when solo cycling is achieved. It's as monumental as Jason Kenny winning his sixth gold.

 Don't... pick a steep downhill to begin the teaching.

If you thought the bike was expensive, wait until you see the chiropractor bill.

Just like when Zayn left One Direction, going solo is a frightening but exciting prospect and Dads need to judge the perfect time to remove their hand from behind the saddle and watch junior cruise by himself.

Up to this point, Dad may well have never told a lie to his child. But when the little 'un screams out "don't let go!" and he replies "I won't", it's a blatant falsity he must live with for the rest of his life. But if it means his kid can finally be classed as a cyclist, he's happy to dish out the lies left, right and centre. Left, right and centre will also probably be the haphazard route the pair take around the park.

Top cycling tips

- Both wear a helmet. Dad's sure to take a tumble too.

- Don't think it'll be fun to have a ride on the little bike yourself. You'll get injured.

- Avoid the dog poo.

#taketoswimming

There's a 'funny' saying that what parents spend on swimming lessons over their child's first eight to ten years, they could have built their own luxury pool and taught him or her how to swim themselves. "Yes, ha-ha, very funny…" grimaces Dad.

Joking aside, it's vital that children are taught how to swim and be comfortable and confident around water from an early age. Inevitably, this means weekly trips to the pool and the rigmarole of packing, undressing, changing, drying, wet hair, wet socks and wet everything else. Even though lessons only last for 30 minutes, the operation takes a whole morning or afternoon. To make matters worse, Dad has to get his hairy feet out poolside or be forced to stick on those awful bright plastic bags to cover his shoes. That's not funny for him or the poor unfortunate onlookers.

CHECKLIST

Do… grab a drink from the coffee shop while you wait. You've earned it.

Don't… forget the costume and make them swim in their underwear.

Top tip

- Whether you have a boy or a girl, go to swimming lessons with the costume already underneath their clothes. It's a total time-saver. Why not even take them with just their dressing gown over the top? Minutes will be shaved from the changing room fiasco.

#getkidsdressed

We all love a pyjama day. Go on, admit it! It's great fun not to get dressed all day, and eat breakfast, lunch and dinner in your Spiderman t-shirt and stripy bottoms. Kids love it too. While that might be fun and fine on a sleepy Sunday in January, most days require the kids to throw on clothes in readiness for school, nursery or being dropped off at nanny's. Dad, remember to change out of that Spidey top if you're involved in any of these activities.

Kids will quite happily wear the same clothes until it's physically impossible to fit inside them. The concept of dirty garments is alien to them. Likewise a Postman Pat or Frozen t-shirt, mixed with shorts and wellies, to them is deemed totally acceptable attire for any occasion. This is where Dad steps in and retrieves jeans, leggings and jumpers from the back of the wardrobe and helps to get toddlers dressed in the morning in under two minutes flat. While he also gets dressed and checks the footy news on his phone at the same time. What a man.

CHECKLIST

 Do...colour coordinate the children. 'Blue and green should never be seen' and all that.

 Don't...forget that, after dressing, the 'three brush rule' must be applied: brush hair, brush teeth and brush soggy Rice Krispies off their clothes.

School Dadmin

You need to be prepped and planned for this stage.

The first four and a bit years of your child's existence is behind you now. Ahead lies the long, long stretch of at least 11 years of school time. Feels great, doesn't it? Read on for an important lesson in what to expect – take notes or you'll be in Dadmin detention!

#dotheschoolrun

Every school day begins with the walk, drive or desperate dash to the school gates. That's not totally accurate, as it actually begins with manic breakfast eating, hair brushing, teeth brushing and lost shoe finding. But once Dad and his kids are out of the house, the countdown's on until the moment you reach school and wave bye-bye for the next six and a half hours.

However prepped and planned Dad is, the daily drop-off is always a race against the clock. The journey is fraught with fear that you've forgotten the PE kit, lunchbox, reading book or one of your children. Dad knows things are really not going his way when he finally turns up at school, only to realise it's a Bank Holiday Monday.

Lastly, it's important Dad understands that although six and a half hours is a long time, in the context of a school day those 390 minutes zoom by in what seems like just an hour and a half. As soon as the school bell rings at 8.45am, it's time to do it all again and turn around to collect the kids. Fear not – by July your school run routine will be textbook.

CHECKLIST

 Do... time how long it takes to get from your front door to the school gates, then try to set a new PB each term.

 Don't... waste time chatting to parents in the playground. Get in and out ASAP.

#makethepacklunch

What children want in their school packed lunch box...

- jam sandwich (crust off)
- Frazzles
- leftover Easter egg
- a big sausage
- cocktail sausages
- apple (red one)
- custard creams
- bottle of cola
- cola bottle sweets
- Lego mini figure toy

What children actually end up with in their school packed lunch box...

- standard ham/cheese sandwich (crust on)
- quinoa-based crisps
- carrot sticks
- healthy fruit sweet
- leftover cheese from Christmas
- apple (any colour)
- random crumbs and cling film
- Lego mini figure toy

As these contrasting lists show, it can be a struggle to pack a lunch box that children will want to consume in the school dinner hall. And if Dad's in charge of the packing, the temptation is always there to take the nice stuff meant for the kids, like chocolate treat bars and yummy yoghurts, and stick it in his own work pack-up box. Well, you can't take quinoa crisps to the office, can you? You can't even pronounce the word.

#helponschooltrip

Once or twice during the school year, Mums and Dads will be forced to volunteer to help on a school trip. Sadly, this means that the six and a half hours when you normally get a break from looking after your own children, turns into eight hours of constant supervision of at least ten kids you've never clapped eyes on before.

Mum has, rather wisely, already done her school trip duty back in the warmth of September, so it's now Dad's turn to step up to the plate for the muddy woods walk in January. Most schools have a policy of not allowing parents to be in charge of their own children during trips, so why not make the day more interesting by inventing a new persona for yourself and share it with the group? When the inquisitive nine-year-olds ask who you are and what job you do, tell them you're a secret agent called Max Power. The kids will think you're super cool. Just hope that none of the class saw The Simpsons episode when Homer changed his name to Max Power and acted like a big-time idiot.

CHECKLIST

 Do... stock up on pencils and fridge magnets in the gift shop.

 Don't...forget to take a headache tablet before the trip.

#attendparentsevening

Going to your child's parents' evening can be an event for both Mum and Dad. But if Dad's despatched to the school by himself, he'll be determined to make the occasion much more than a mere check up on reading, writing and arithmetic.

Firstly, he'll spend ages talking and joking about how small the classroom chairs are and that he can't believe how he sat on such a small seat himself back in the day. And look at how low down the sinks and coat pegs are! Amazing. When one-on-one with the teacher, with his child beside him, Dad will just naturally say awkward things and ask nonsense questions which are totally embarrassing for the kid. After all, it's what his Dad did to him years ago, so it's only fair he passes on the parents' evening pain to his own flesh and blood. 'Must try harder' to act normal, you could say about yourself.

CHECKLIST

 Do...take an interest in your child's schoolwork and books.

 Don't... take a newspaper to help pass the time.

She's easily distracted.

Sorry, what was that?

#helpwithhomework

In the eyes of his kids, Dad can become an instant hero in the homework stakes. If he's able to glue yoghurt pots and cereal boxes together at the kitchen table to create the International Space Station, his kid will be top of the class in Science topic. On the other hand, if he knows naff all about long division and inverse equations, his little 'un won't be impressed and will suddenly realise that Dad isn't the smartest tool in the shed. You don't need to be a rocket surgeon to work that out.

So, Dads have a tendency to blag most homework tasks they get involved with. Obviously Google is a big help in things like naming Henry VIII's seven, or six, wives and what Europe's major capital cities are. If technology fails him, he'll need to trot out the famous line: "ask your Mum, because she's good at stuff like that." Hopefully, Mum hasn't already declared to your child: "ask your Dad, because he's good at stuff like that."

CHECKLIST

 Do... get homework done nice and early.

 Don't... instruct your kid to tell the teacher that the dog ate their homework.

#sortschoolbag

Socks, wellies, apples, books, hats, gloves, letters, money, cheese straws and Nerf blasters. These are all random items that can be found in a child's schoolbag. No father is able to dodge the school Dadmin duty of sorting and packing his son or daughter's rucksack. And yes, at some point he'll have to reach in to fish out the sweaty PE sock from the bottom of it.

It's vital to work out the safe carrying load of a school rucksack. Packing in spare clothes, lunch box, trainers and coats is only fine if the bag's primary user can support such a shipment. That, of course, refers to Dad. No savvy six or seven-year-old carries their own bag to school when it can be thrown onto a father's shoulders. Pink flowery patterns, Captain America or Minecraft – whatever style bag it is, Dads literally have to be able to carry it off.

CHECKLIST

☑ *Do... use extra school bags if needed.*

☒ *Don't... use ASDA carrier bags. Kids can't bear the 5p shame of it.*

#**doafterschoolclub**

There's only one thing better than an afterschool club or activity, and that's a free afterschool club or activity. It's not that parents are desperate to hold off having to pick their children up from school, but the extra hour that their child spends doing gymnastics, football or playground litter picking is much more beneficial to them as individuals. If it just happens to mean that Mums and Dads miss the school gate rush and have time to grab a coffee from Waitrose, then that's a happy coincidence.

Getting children to take part in an afterschool club can be tricky. In pleasant months like June, July and September, kids are only too happy to spend extra time outside in gardening or athletics club. Through November to March, it takes a bit more convincing that they should join Mrs Fletcher's hockey class or be part of school rugby training. Indoor clubs, like craft and cooking, can become oversubscribed during these dark times and Dads must be quick to sign them up straight away.

At the end of the day, afterschool clubs are very rewarding for kids and parents at the, er, end of the day.

CHECKLIST

 Do... get your children involved in a range of activities.

 Don't... ask the school to set up weekend-long afterschool clubs.

#findschooluniform

School uniform seems to have the power to disappear and hide by itself. This may be because of supersized bacteria formed from tuna sandwich and toothpaste stains. Or, more likely, because kids throw it behind the sofa or TV each afternoon and no-one thinks about its whereabouts until 8.15am the next day. Dads must be ready to be deployed on uniform retrieval missions at the drop of a hat. Or the drop of a blue blazer and matching tie.

Every piece of uniform needs to be correctly named and tagged because, at some point, it'll vanish into the playground ether. This usually results in a trip to the lost property box and the lucky dip to find lost garments. Nametags can be neatly stitched into clothing. Equally, surnames can be scribbled on labels with permanent marker in about 20 seconds and with much less stabbing of fingers with needles.

In all honesty, parents should be grateful for the existence of school uniform. The alternative is five days of non-uniform, which usually cost Mum and Dad two quid per day for the PTA coffers.

CHECKLIST

 Do... *make uniforms last until the last day of the summer term.*

Don't... *expect stain remover to remove school uniform stains. Ever.*

#winsportsdayrace

Every child thinks that their Dad's stronger than The Rock, faster than The Flash and more athletic than The Team GB Olympic Squad. With this expectation weighing heavy on his not-very-sporty shoulders, Dad takes part in the school sports day each summer. It's an event that he pretends to take nonchalantly, but in secret he's been doing press-ups every morning and eating Special K instead of Frosties.

The pinnacle event is the sports field sprint. It's easy to spot the Dads who have come prepared, wearing new trainers and loose fitting gear instead of their usual workboots and skinny jeans. At the starting line, after the head teacher drops the flag, Dads set off in pursuit of racing glory. After just 12 metres and a pulled hamstring and twisted knee, Dads will painfully limp to the line and joke that it's all just a bit of fun really, isn't it? Looking across at their distraught son or daughter, he'll soon realise that, in their eyes, he's not even at the level of the weedy man from the Mr Muscle TV adverts.

CHECKLIST

 Do... cheer on your children in their events.

 Don't... critique their poor technique in the three-legged race.

Winner

#surviveschoolholidays

You and your partner have been counting down the days in dread. There it is, marked on the calendar in big, bold red letters – SCHOOL HOLIDAYS. When it arrives, there's no hiding. The beginning of the school hols means that your support mechanism has been taken away from you, and suddenly, you're the one having to keep kids entertained, busy and safe all day. At times like these, parents appreciate what a good, and slightly crazy, bunch of people teachers really are.

Surviving a half term week, Christmas and Easter is a breeze compared to the scary six-week summer break. Just sorting a six-week stint of childcare, babysitting and work-leave takes about six weeks in itself. It then requires six weeks to recover and recuperate when the kids go back in September, which takes you up to the October half-term break and all the fun begins again.

CHECKLIST

 Do... take the kids on fun days out.

 Don't... cry on day one of the school holidays.

School holiday survival strategy

- If Mum and Dad are both around, tag-team it and each be in charge of the kids for 60 minutes, max, at a time. Teamwork is the way.

Dadmin
Forever

These are your classic Dadmin duties.

From dealing with spiders to trips to the dump, building flatpack furniture and venturing into the loft – the evergreen dad jobs, regardless of family size, your age or if you secretly are an arachnophobe.

The next wodge of pages will steer you through your staple list of Dadmin tasks. Paint brushes, sponges, screwdrivers and measuring tapes at the ready, fellas...

#mowthelawn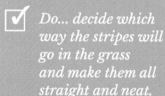

This is your big chance to turn your turf into something that looks like Wembley on cup final day. In reality, it may end up looking more like a National Trust vegetable patch than a national football pitch, but technically the grass length is now shorter than it was, so job done.

Mowing the lawn is a time-honoured tradition. Your Dad and your Grandad did it, with a petrol-powered monster louder than a Kawasaki 125, so your electric beauty from B&Q (£39.99) will have no probs. The only problem you may encounter will be harnessing electricity so that your machine will reach the bottom of the garden – using a three-metre extension cable is never a good idea. So, nip back to B&Q for a 30 metre one that means you could, if you wanted, cut Mrs Murray's grass at No14 without unplugging.

CHECKLIST

☑️ *Do... decide which way the stripes will go in the grass and make them all straight and neat.*

☒ *Don't... give up on the stripes idea halfway through and wave the mower around like a metal detector.*

Top Tips

- Take as long as you want cutting the grass. It can take 15 minutes or two hours, depending on whatever else you're trying to avoid doing that day.

- Remove any lawn obstacles prior to cutting. Leaving a Peppa Pig space hopper shape behind isn't a good look.

#fixeverything

Things break. Things need fixing. That's been a rule of life ever since 'things' were first invented. If a caveman's spear snapped, he had to fix it or he wouldn't harpoon many fish that day.

After Dad weighs up the potential time required for the fixing task – two minutes, two hours or two days looking for help on YouTube – he will then prepare himself mentally and physically for the repair mission in front of him. Mental prep is important if you're fixing something like a dodgy toaster or blocked Dyson, whereas you'll need to warm your muscles up if your job is to tackle the broken fence after damage caused by Storm Brian. Or was it Storm Dorothy? Maybe it was Eleanor, or Emma or....

Tools are important, obviously. While the most vital tools will always be Dad's delightfully dexterous digits (i.e. his fingers) and his brain that's pre-wired into problem-solving mode, a Phillips screwdriver, hammer and pliers are helpful too.

CHECKLIST

 Do... the most challenging fixes first. 'Fix the things that count, not count the things you fix', as a wise Dad once said.

 Don't... go OTT and wear overalls just to screw a cupboard door back on.

Phillips screwdriver?
But you don't even have
a mate called Phillip...?

Even a simple fix, like replacing batteries, can require a screwdriver to remove the cover and pop those double AAs out. Never be ashamed to use a lot of tools to fix something. This demonstrates the severity of your work and the professional approach you have adopted. Hopefully, what it doesn't demonstrate is that in order to fix a relatively simple problem, you've somehow created a much bigger problem and therefore had to use more tools than even Bob the Builder can manage.

When everything is finally fixed, stand back and admire your achievement. Admittedly, unclogging the vacuum or removing Lego from the DVD player isn't much to crow about, but it could still be crossed off the 'Dadmin to do' list. And if the fence survives the next gust of wind (Storm Keith?) then you can be double pleased.

*5 things to
(constantly) fix*

1. Bikes

2. Toilets

3. Radiators

4. Shelves

5. Doors

#getridofspiders

Take a look at your surroundings. You're standing in your lounge/kitchen/kid's bedroom and faced with the Dadmin duty of removing a little house spider. You're not in the Australian Outback, sweat dripping as you attempt to tackle a tarantula. Dads in the UK should be mightily grateful for having such an easy ride compared to the father folk Down Under.

Carefully catching a spider inside your house and placing it safely outside is a routine scenario. You can take one of two options; go freehand and grab it, or opt for the more popular technique of glass and piece of paper. If you pick it up with your bare hands then you'll do quite well if you're ever invited to a Bushtucker Trial. But there's nothing degrading about placing a glass over the spider and sliding paper underneath to trap it. This way, you get to have a close-up look at the spider before dropping him off in the garden. Now, do they have six or eight legs? One, two, three...

CHECKLIST

 Do... tell yourself 'the spider is more afraid of you than you are of him'.

 Don't... actually believe that. You'll always be just a little bit more afraid.

#takerubbishout

This is, of course, a completely necessary Dadmin assignment, but completely mind-numbing too. No enjoyment can ever be garnered from taking the rubbish out. All you're doing is moving one pile of rubbish from inside to a bigger pile of rubbish outside. Then, once a week, wheeling that big pile of rubbish to a place where it'll be thrown in with an even bigger pile of rubbish and taken away by people in hi-vis clothing. Nothing spectacular or special in that. No sir.

Surprisingly, there's a fair amount of knowledge required in a successful rubbish removal routine. What goes in which bin? Are egg boxes recyclable? What day are the bins collected? And that's without the added confusion of Bank Holidays and the immense impact this can have on a bin collection schedule. Leave it to Dad and he'll sort it, but if he doesn't, luckily there's a contingency plan on the next page...

CHECKLIST

 Do... give the bins a good wash if they stink worse than smelly armpits and burnt cabbage.

 Don't... forget to tip the bin men at Christmas. It pays off in the long run.

Top tips

- It's illegal to put bins out more than 12 hours before they're due for collection. Okay it's not, but it should be.

- Stashing stuff in next door's bin is fine, as long as they don't see you.

- Never take bins out wearing your onesie.

#takerubbishtodump

When the standard wheelie bin and rubbish collection service isn't up to the job, a Dad is then faced with a trip to the dump. This can be both a frightening and exciting excursion. Loading the car with bits of carpet, black bin bags and broken garden chairs makes you feel like you're on an army mission, transporting vital supplies to a secret drop-off. When actually, it's midday on the first sunny Saturday of the year and every other Dad in your area will ram their Renault Scenic with random rubbish and join you down at the dump.

Upon driving into your dump, you should try to stay calm and relaxed. You've got this covered. Even the fact the place is now called the Household Recycling and Rejuvenation Centre for Disused and Discarded Matter shouldn't make you grind your teeth.

CHECKLIST

☑ *Do... call everyone 'mate' at the dump. You'll feel great and very manly.*

☒ *Don't... put MDF with the wood waste. It's not the same (even oak veneered MDF, apparently).*

Cardboard must be not made of card and must be flat but not flattened.

Throw your rubbish as far as your manly muscles will allow.

Nice one mate.

But then, as you open your boot, panic sets in. You realise you have no idea what's in the black bin bags! Is it general waste? Plastic? Cardboard for recycling? Is sparkly Christmas wrapping paper even recyclable? Plus, you're not sure if broken garden chairs go with plastic or metal waste. Argh!

You have no choice but to ask the staff at the Household Recycling and Rejuvenation Centre for Disused and Discarded Matter for help. Making you feel just a little bit pathetic, they sort through your bags and send you off to each waste container you need. Even your act of bravado in carrying the carpet backfires, as the staff, once again, have to help you lift it into the container. Console yourself in the knowledge you won't go back there for another year. Or four.

Dump rules

- Like the SAS, get in and out quickly. The optimum time to spend at the dump is two minutes 27 seconds.

- Take maximum pleasure in smashing, bashing and throwing fragile things into the containers.

Do not fill

Do Fill

Middle man

Time for a break from all that Dadmin.

Good stuff – you've reached the middle of this book! To celebrate, why not try some of these things when you're slap bang in the middle of your classic Dadmin jobs?

Have a cup of tea. It's a cliché of course, but worth every sip.

Halfway through one bit of Dadmin, try starting another. Your wife says you can't multitask, but you'll prove you can gloss skirting AND check Whatsapp.

Check Facebook.

Grab a snack. There's no rush to finish your Dadmin — you have the whole Bank Holiday weekend, after all.

Take a Dadmin selfie. Be proud that the shelf you're putting up is nearly almost level.

Check Whatsapp.

Have another cup of tea.

#dotheshopping

The term 'doing the shopping' could mean many things. It could mean shopping for a cool new TV. Or that pair of trainers you quite fancy, and that t-shirt you really like. Yes, it could mean all of those, but you know it doesn't. In 98.76 per cent of times, when a Dad's challenged to do the shopping, it means trudging to Tesco or Aldi and filling bags with items that feed and keep the family happy for another seven days.

Generally, Dads prefer to do this alone. The shopping is done quicker and he can pick up essentials like cookies, doughnuts and Turtle Wax car shampoo. You could be a Dad who's methodical in his shopping style. This means navigating the trolley around the aisles in the same direction each week, stopping periodically to check you have everything on your list and that the eggs aren't squashed under 10kg of washing powder.

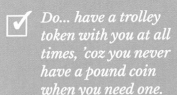

CHECKLIST

☑ *Do... have a trolley token with you at all times, 'coz you never have a pound coin when you need one.*

☒ *Don't...stand on the back of the trolley and zoom down the aisle when no one is looking. Tsk.*

Always remember to write a list before you go shopping. In case you are the forgetful type, write a note now to remind you to write a list.

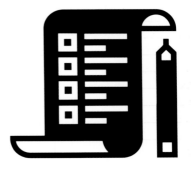

The other type of Dad will race through the supermarket as if he's on a sponsored trolley dash, grabbing things he probably thinks are needed. This speedy shopper has no call for a shopping list – to him, lists are for losers. It's a risky strategy but he backs himself to deliver the goods each time. And the baked beans and loo roll.

Supermarket shopping with the whole family is a different ball game. It adds on an extra 38 minutes (at least) and the trolley fills up with extra yoghurts, crisps and hairspray. You're conscious of only having 90 minutes of free parking and your choice of which checkout queue to join suddenly becomes monumental. If the old couple in front of you pay their £34.76 bill entirely with the 20p coins they've saved, you'll never get the ice cream home in time.

Shopping tips

- If you can't find an item, please ask for assistance. Taking an hour to spot ginger extract is not productive.

- Get your weekly shop in just a basket. It's cheaper and gives you arms like The Hulk.

- Selecting a trolley with wheels that move forwards, and not only sideways, can be a problem.

#cleanthecar

This is what Saturday mornings/Saturday afternoons/ Sunday mornings/Sunday afternoons are made for, yeah? First things first, these pages deal with ACTUALLY CLEANING THE CAR YOURSELF. Driving to the car wash and paying someone £9.50 to do it, while you peer through the windscreen sipping a Starbucks, does not qualify as ACTUALLY CLEANING THE CAR YOURSELF. Roll up your sleeves (literally) and get stuck in.

Dad's aim here is very simple: make a dirty car clean. This can be as straight forward or as complicated as you like. If you're planning on just a five-minute frenzy to spruce up the family five-door, have a hosepipe, sponge and chamois leather at the ready. Quickly run the sponge all over, rinse, apply the chamois and you'll be done and dusted* in no time. If, though, you have a leisurely couple of hours to invest in this particular Dadmin, then it could be time to unleash your A game... polishing!

CHECKLIST

 Do... spend an afternoon choosing cleaning products at Halfords.

 Don't... use one of the kid's bath sponges.

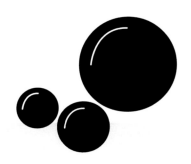

Yep, if you're really going to do this properly, then applying gunky circles to the bodywork, followed by more manic circular movements with a separate cloth, is the only way. However, once you've managed to polish the top half of one door, you're so bored that waxing the entire car seems like total torture. At this point you discreetly pack away your polishing kit. It's going to chuck it down in the next 30 seconds anyway.

And what about the inside of the car? No one from the outside can see the inside, so does it need vacuuming and wiping? In the end, Dads often use the technique of rummaging around the seats and floor mats to remove the more unsightly lumps of mud, mouldy chocolate, crisp packets and, er, Starbucks cups.

* WARNING: dusting your car with a rainbow extendable feather duster is not a good idea.

Dodge it in Deutschland

If you really hate having to clean the car, then you should move to Germany. In some towns and cities, it's illegal to wash it at home because chemicals can drain into the water system. If that sounds appealing, you'd better start packing your bags for Berlin...

#takecartogarage

On the subject of cars, a couple of times a year yours will have to be taken to the local garage for an MOT, servicing, repairs and because it makes an odd noise in second gear when you turn left on cold days. For Dads, the garage and dealing with car-fixing folk is a tricky test to navigate. It's a chance to appear very knowledgeable amidst talk of anti-roll bar linkage ball joints and carburettors. But then again, all the technical spiel can just go over your head as you really have no idea where the spare tyre is or even how to open the bonnet.

Rightly so, Dads will try to make as many car repairs themselves at home (see 'tinkering' on page 73) before giving up and being forced to pay fifty quid an hour labour charge. Grrr.

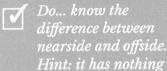

CHECKLIST

✔ *Do... know the difference between nearside and offside. Hint: it has nothing to do with football.*

✗ *Don't... expect repairs to be made in under 30 minutes. Kwik Fit is the most ironic business name ever.*

Frustrated that you can't replace a simple windscreen wiper, stick a new indicator bulb in or work out why the seat won't slide back, your only option is to hand the keys over to Mike and the mechanics. Then what do you do? Wait anxiously at the garage for hours? Garages have that MOT viewing area where you can stand and watch your car being pulled apart and bashed by hammers and drills, but that's often more painful than paying the bill. Best to leave the scene and wait for the call to collect it.

Whether you have a knackered old Nissan or a flashy new Ford, trips to the garage are unavoidable for Dads. Never mind though, at least you're capable of topping up the bright blue windscreen washer. Well, you would be if you actually knew how to open the bonnet.

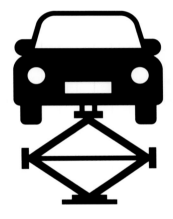

I need to loosen your nuts.

Will that hurt?

#buildsomeflatpack

The year was 1987. The setting was Manchester. The event was IKEA's first store opening in the UK. Historians may mark this as the start of changing consumer trends that would forever shape the future of home furniture retail on these isles. For Dads, the year had much more significance: flat pack had entered their world, destined never to leave.

In the 21st century, flat pack is as much an important part of Dad's life as walking, eating, breathing oxygen and watching Strictly. Whatever piece of furniture you admire in a shop or on a website, be it a wardrobe, bookcase, TV unit or extending kitchen table, your mind will always fast forward to the day it'll be delivered to your doorstep in a box a mere fraction of the size of your newly-purchased item.

CHECKLIST

 Do... have a schoolboy chuckle at the funny furniture names, like Ektorp, Godmorgen, Gorm and Versam.

 Don't... ever declare "I'll build this in ten minutes." Flat pack adheres to no known space-time dimensions.

Before you're ready to begin your flat pack assembling, you first have to decide if you will actually check all the components are there. Clearly the instructions tell you to do this, but counting all the screws, caps, clips, pins, blocks, brackets, hinges, handles, straps, rails, glues and twisty and turny things is a complete headache. That's without having to separate the screws into categories, checking there are 16 of the 5mm 100215 screw, 25 of the 15mm 102179 type and 48 of those little 100404 fellas. Nope. Looking through the plastic bags of bits and pieces, it appears as though everything's there. Time to advance to the estimated 30-minute task of flat pack construction.

Three hours and 14 minutes later, after your entire family has been roped in to help hold shelves, adjust hinges and search under the sofa for a mislaid 100404, your work is done. You've conquered the flat pack yet again. Well done, you.

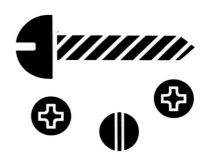

Flat pack facts

- IKEA has sold over 41 million of its ridiculously popular BILLY bookcases. That equates to 27.2 trillion hours of flat pack assembling. Probably.

- The Allen key was invented by a man called Allen. Well, a man called William G. Allen, actually.

#paintsomething

Van Gogh, Picasso, Rembrandt – and that bloke who took quite a long time to colour in a church ceiling – were wonderfully talented artists. You, sadly, don't have as much talent with a paintbrush in your hand. But, armed with the achievement that you did manage to paint the kitchen in just six weeks, you'll don your overalls and take on another task.

Preparation is the key to a good splash of Dadmin painting. If it takes you twice as long to arrange your brushes, tins, groundsheets and cups of tea than actually doing the job, then so be it. When you're ready, whip out your new roller, run it through the paint tray and start covering the walls in apple white. After daubing your initials six times for a laugh, you'll soon take it seriously.

CHECKLIST

 Do... put on cheesy loud music. It's a scientific fact that blasting out Justin Bieber tunes while a Dad paints, increases his productivity.

 Don't... decide on the colour by yourself. Just don't take that risk. Ever.

#dothewashingup

This is one of the most mundane missions in this Dadmin manual. There's no getting away from it – unless the kids fancy eating Weetabix in a colander using barbeque tongs, dad's gonna have to wash up the bowls and cutlery at some point. The only escape is to get a dishwasher, but that brings the misery of loading and emptying it. Plus, even Mr Bosch and Mr Zanussi don't really know what to do with dishwasher salt granules.

Most Dads opt to tackle a 'job lot' of washing up all at once. Why spend just a couple of minutes doing it a few times a day, when one mammoth 50-minute session takes care of everything? Another benefit of this approach is that you can balance the bundle of pots, pans, plates and Prosecco glasses on the drainer like a crazy adult version of Buckaroo. Fun for all the family!

CHECKLIST

 Do... allow a dirty pan 'to soak'. Return to it three hours later and see how it will have magically cleaned itself. And floated back into its cupboard.

 Don't... use pink rubber gloves. Yellow ones are fine, though.

Washing up rules

- Adhere to a strict rota where family members take it in turns to wash up, but Dad still seems to be left doing it on any day ending in 'y'.

- You can use a scouring pad for really gritty stains, but never sandpaper.

#putstuffintheloft

Going in the loft is not something a Dad ever likes doing. We all dream of having a fancy spiral staircase leading to a converted soundproof space packed with TV screens, corner sofas and Scalextric sets. In reality, the loft's a dark and uninviting place – a bit like Blackpool in January – that's either freezing cold or boiling hot. A bit like Blackpool again then, just not the boiling hot bit. But, years of practise of dropping the ladder down without slicing any fingers off means it's a job for Dad and Dad alone. Plus you know exactly where everything is up there. Sort of.

Early Dadmin folk may make the mistake of climbing the ladder sans footwear. That's a schoolboy error. Going into the loft is strictly a trainers/slippers/Crocs on situation, 'coz those metal steps are painful and cold.

CHECKLIST

☑ *Do... look out for scary things like spiders, mice and your embarrassing school photos.*

☒ *Don't... touch the loft insulation. It's itchier than a 1970s woolly jumper.*

With many hundreds of loft excursions under your belt, you can locate the light switch within 30 seconds (usually) and begin the vital task of putting that box of Christmas napkins and coasters away. You try to remember which floorboards are safe to stand on, which roof rafters will really hurt if you bang into them, and find a space to store the box.

You'll always have to navigate past a giant cardboard box from a Sony 36-inch you bought in 2012. Your mind will wander as you imagine how cool it would be to have a TV in the loft, but we all know that's a distant dream. Now you can wander back over to the loft hatch, avoiding obstacles in a manner best described as a cross between Neil Armstrong's moonwalk and an Olympic hurdler, and begin your descent.

Top loft tips

- Remember you're not Peter Crouch and you can NEVER reach the loft ladder from the landing without a stool. Bless.

- You're the only person who goes in the loft. Make as much mess as you like, but always comment on how tidy it is to the family. The joke's on them.

#measurestuff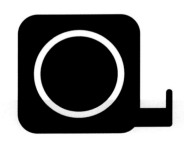

Admittedly, most kids begin to measure stuff when they're about four years old. But Dads measure important things such as radiator widths and room lengths with a proper tape measure. Kids measure how long a worm in the garden is using their little finger.

The best thing about having to measure is the tape measure itself – one of the funkiest and most multi-purpose tools on the planet. It will perform its basic task very well by easily stretching between two points to calculate a distance. More importantly, though, if the tape is extended a little bit it can act as a toy gun and a backscratcher. Then there's the wonderful game of seeing how far a Dad can extend the tape horizontally or at an upward angle, before it finally gives way and bends. That fun can go on for a 'long' time! Sorry.

Just be careful when you flick the unlock button and it instantly recoils. The tape can come back to you at breakneck, or even breakfinger, speed.

CHECKLIST

☑ *Do... write your measurements down. Try to remember them and you'll just pluck random numbers from midair.*

☒ *Don't... use a 30 cm ruler to measure the length of your kitchen floor.*

#haveatinker

As a Dad, you may think that you never tinker, but take a look at the Dadmin dictionary definition…

Tinker (verb)
to try to improve, repair or mend something in a casual way.
Example usage: "The lawn mower's not working very well, honey. I'll just tinker with it for a bit."

Now will you admit to a little bit of tinkering here and there? Don't be ashamed of fiddling, dabbling, trifling, pottering and playing with stuff. No Dad ever set out to harm any thing or person with his tinkering ways. The purpose is to boost an object's effectiveness or function. The fact that you've spent all morning, and got through two loaves of bread, just to conclude that toaster setting 3 delivers the optimum browning level should be neither here nor there.

CHECKLIST

☑ *Do… feel free to tinker with things in the shed. It's quiet there and you can concentrate.*

☒ *Don't… tinker with more than three things at once. That way madness lies.*

I know it was working perfectly, but I'm just having a tinker to try and make it better.

#drillsomething

This is a biggie. Just like the moment you first heard that Donald Trump had become President Trump, every Dad remembers when he first drilled something. Every Dad also remembers the first time he messed up big-time with his drilling, as the two memories are often combined.

The actual act of drilling is usually over in a few seconds, but pre-drilling requires a much longer run-up. Meticulous measurements must be taken and then re-taken. The correct drill bit type and size needs to be selected and any screws and wall plugs for the job must be at hand, much like how surgeons have their instruments precisely laid out for them.

Drilling into wood is a doddle compared to internal household drilling into solid walls. The general rule is the louder the drilling, the greater the Dadmin task you're undertaking. And the greater the risk of your wall falling down, obviously. But after a bit of practice, you soon get the hang of it and move on from simple picture frames and shelves to the real biggie... making holes to fix up the TV wall bracket. That's the Daddy of all drilling.

CHECKLIST

 Do... have a tub of filler ready to cover all the 'practice' holes you drilled.

Don't... decide to superglue shelves to the wall instead.

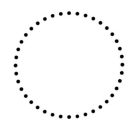

#cookthetea

Come 5.26pm in most UK households, kids will become extremely hungry and irritable and require feeding immediately. If this duty befalls Dad, he must burst into the kitchen and conjure up some gorgeous grub to stop his children from having a mega meltdown. And no, mega meltdown is not the new spicy option on the Domino's menu.

Always keep your kitchen well stocked with basic ingredients like a tin of chopped tomatoes, stock cubes, easy cook rice, eggs, pasta, potatoes and custard. The last item is very important because no matter how awful your main dish may be, serving a vat of sugary yellow stuff for dessert will make your children forget the horrible meal they've just endured.

Confident cooks have no problem taking on something extravagant like a full Sunday roast. These Dads deserve the utmost respect because not only does this mean they're cooking all day Sunday, but have to spend Saturday shopping and prepping for it and half of Monday washing up the roasting tin.

CHECKLIST

 Do... spell out silly words in the frozen Alphabites.

 Don't... let the kids sort their own tea because Cheerios, jaffa cakes and bread is not a meal.

Dad's Top meals

1. Spag bol (once you've tinkered with the recipe)
2. Miscellaneous pasta dish
3. Burgers, ideally on the barbeque
4. Toast
5. Baked beans
6. Baked beans on toast
7. Lasagne
8. That Jamie Oliver Thing
9. Sausage and mash
10. Sunday roast

#changethelightbulb

How many Dads does it take to change a light bulb? You'll find that answer, and more fantastic/terrible Dad jokes on page 110, so let's be serious now, please.

Dads try to play it cool when it comes to changing a light bulb. It's a nice thought that you alone have the power to light up a room, when actually your wife and even teenage offspring are perfectly capable of slotting in a new GU10, MR16 or SES candle. But, do they know what all this coded talk means? Can they work out their lumens from their wattage, or even their equivalent wattage? Nope.

And neither do most Dads, to he honest. These days, buying the appropriate light bulb is much more difficult than fitting the thing. That's why you see dozens of confused blokes standing in the light bulb aisle at B&Q or Homebase, looking completely dazed at what's on display in front of them. At times like these, Dads really can feel like they're left in the dark.

CHECKLIST

 Do... use a stepladder to reach a ceiling bulb, because your coffee table has a dodgy leg.

 Don't... keep a note of whether the bulb will last for 10,000 hours, like it says on the box.

Just popping back to Homebase.

We got the wrong ones, it's got a screw fitting.

#cleanthewindows

Probably the most dangerous household cleaning duty. Well, cleaning the toilet can be a toughie, but there's not much risk of falling from a ladder while doing it.

Dads are only faced with having to clean the outside of the upstairs windows for one reason: they refuse to pay someone with such hi-tech tools as a damp cloth and a squeegee £12 to do it for them. You have your own damp cloth and squeegee, thanks very much.

Squeegee. Is there a funnier word in the English dictionary? It sounds silly every time it comes out of your mouth, and it's even sillier to write. Go on, write it down. How many other words do you know have a quadruple e? It's insane!

Er, getting back on topic… cleaning windows is a Dadmin doddle, as long as your entire family are prepared to hold the bottom of the ladder each time you venture up it.

CHECKLIST

☑ *Do... decide to live in a bungalow just to avoid cleaning upstairs windows.*

☒ *Don't... ever think you'll stop saying 'squeegee' for the rest of the day now.*

Top window cleaning tip

Pay a window cleaner to do it.

#filltheskip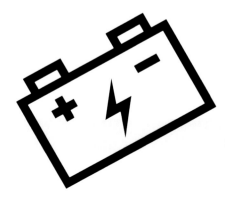

Taking the rubbish out, going to the dump; the final piece of Dadmin to complete the Holy Trinity of filthy tasks is filling a skip at home. But listen Dads, don't sigh because having a skip on your drive means three things...

1. You won't be making 27 car trips to the dump. Good times.
2. You can make lots of noise and throw things around.
3. Your neighbours will know you're doing big time Dadmin that requires more than a wheelie bin and a black plastic bag.

Firstly, what size skip to order? You need one big enough for whatever your clearing job is (the small skips just look like luminous shopping baskets) and just the right size to cause next door to have to park their BMW on the road. Once the skip's been dropped, you can begin the job of loading it up by shoving in all the waste you can lay your hands on.

CHECKLIST

☑ *Do... guard your skip like it's the crown jewels.*

☒ *Don't... jump up and down on it in an effort to pack stuff down. It's not a bouncy castle.*

Skip jumping is not a good idea. Last year 961 Dads were (probably) admitted to hospital with skip jumping related injuries.

It's at this point, upon inspecting the skip's contents, that your nosey neighbours will realise that you're not doing something glamorous, like installing a swimming pool, but merely slinging out the kids' old trampoline, swing and playhouse. Plus the busted bits of fence. And that broken toilet that's been in the garage since 2011.

The neighbourly interventions won't stop there. As you're filling up the skip, several will wander over and happen to mention they have an old mattress and a battery from a Fiat Panda to dispose of. At this point you either instruct them to help themselves and join in the skip-filling festivities, or charge them ten quid per item they want to chuck in. At this rate that swimming pool dream could become a reality.

Can I pop this in your skip?

Sure, just give me a tenner.

SHED RULES

RULE 1:

The shed is Dad's shed.
Even if it's full of children's bikes,
toys, a sand pit and inflatable paddling
pool, it's still technically Dad's shed.

RULE 2:

It shall not be questioned **if Dad**
wants to run an extension lead to
the shed and power an electric
heater all day so he can
remain in there.

RULE 3:

A shed that has electrical sockets **is a very fancy shed indeed.**

RULE 4:

In Dad's eyes, building your own shed is as manly as wrestling a crocodile.

RULE 5:

Painting a shed misty grey with a seaside blue door instantly turns it into a summerhouse.

RULE 6:

The key to the shed padlock shall be kept in a secret place where only Dad knows. The kids should never reveal to Dad that under the plant pot is not very secret.

RULE 7:

If Dad shouts from within his shed on a Saturday afternoon, his team are either losing or he's having a particular DIY problem. Do not approach in either scenario.

RULE 8:

If Dad is diagnosed with shed envy caused by another Dad's shed, the only cure is for him to upgrade his own shed.

Teenage Dadmin

Prepare for a traumatic six years.

DO NOT *Teenager's room* **ENTER!**

This bit should really have been on page 13, just to ram home the significance of your child turning 13. Get ready as you deal with moody offspring, arguments, WiFi wars, hellish family excursions and bedrooms looking like bombsites.

#bethetaxi

This was never part of Dad's career plan. But, he now finds himself becoming a full-time taxi driver because his teenager demands to be driven to town, the bowling alley and to friends' houses all the time. You'll know you really are a cabbie when your son or daughter messages you with their bookings and pick up/drop off times each week.

It's a difficult Dadmin duty to get out of. On the one hand you want your teen to have a social life and see their friends, but on the other, you'd like to see the four walls in your lounge every now and then. Plus, you can't charge them for petrol as they'll just ask for more pocket money to cover it. It's Catch 22. And as for suggesting they catch the bus, forget about it…

CHECKLIST

 Do… remember that, ultimately, you want your child to get to their destination safely.

 Don't… forget to record Match of the Day while you're out.

Can you pick me up at 11pm Dad?

Sure, I have no life of my own now.

Top taxi tips

Make the journey uncomfortable, in the hope they'll call for your taxi service less in the future. Tips include playing Take That loudly with the windows down and discussing Brexit in detail with them.

#askteenagertotidybedroom

Teenagers don't tidy their bedroom. Or tidy anything or anywhere.

Times Dad has asked teenager to tidy bedroom (twelve month period)

卌 卌 卌 卌 卌 卌 卌 卌 卌 卌 卌 卌 卌
卌 卌 卌 卌 卌 卌 卌 卌 卌 卌 卌 卌 卌
卌 卌 卌 卌 卌 卌 卌 卌 卌 卌 卌 卌 卌

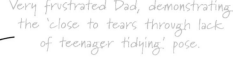

Very frustrated Dad, demonstrating the 'close to tears through lack of teenager tidying' pose.

Deal with it.

#givethepocketmoney

The Bank of Dad really kicks in during the teenage years. This is somewhat strange because, from about 15 onwards, kids can actually get part-time jobs and buy their own hairspray and Haribo without pestering parents for handouts.

Teenagers can forget most things. They generally have no idea what time school starts and how to put clothes in the laundry basket, but they can always remember whether or not they've had their pocket money each week. They can also recall exactly how long the current pay structure has been in place, and do their best Robert Peston impression to argue that pocket money has failed to keep pace with the rate of inflation.

Dad's only hope of getting proper value for money is to come up with a list of chores to be completed before begrudgingly handing out a fiver. If his kids want him to cash out, then they'd better get the vacuum and duster out first.

CHECKLIST

 Do... insist that five quid can go a long way (in Poundland).

 Don't... try to fob them off with 50p. It's not 1994.

Twenty Quid! In 1994 I could buy 100 half penny sweets with 50p

#funfamilytrip

Taking a teenager out for a family trip to the seaside means three things;

1. They have to get out of bed.
2. They'll be away from their iPad or Xbox.
3. They have to be within five metres of you for most of the day.

On the rare occasion that all three of these occur and your teenager joins Mum and Dad at the coast, you now have to keep him or her happy for the day. This can be achieved in a variety of ways, but generally buying food and drink and giving extra pocket money are top of the list. Dads shouldn't take it personally when the teenager spends more time looking at their phone than looking and talking to him. The best thing is just to text your child to ask if they want another ice cream as that way you'll be sure to get a response.

CHECKLIST

 Do... talk about the fun times you had at the beach when you were a lad.

 Don't... think your kids will enjoy listening to your seaside stories.

Teenage tip

- Just accept that they like to wear hoodies all the time, whether it's -4°C or 34°C.

#fixthewifi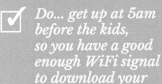

On a simple level, human beings have very basic needs – food, water, shelter, warmth, oxygen and sleep rank right up there. For teenagers though, 24-hour access to high-speed WiFi comes before all of these, with sleep second and 5GB of mobile data a close third. In their eyes, a house with no WiFi is as much use as a tin of tuna with no tin opener. It's Dad's job to pay for and maintain the home router and keep the broadband in full working order.

On the face of it, keeping the WiFi running should be straightforward Dadmin, but it comes with a heap of pressure. When it's working, the world seems a happy place. But the moment it drops out, the bottom of Dad's world seems to drop out too.

CHECKLIST

☑ *Do... get up at 5am before the kids, so you have a good enough WiFi signal to download your work emails.*

☒ *Don't... become one of those nerdy Dads who test the broadband speed daily.*

What's the wifi code again?

Try switching the power off and on.
If it fixes it, this still counts
as a big Dadmin win.

That's not because he's suddenly denied access to Netflix or Sky Sports, but because he's then faced with the prospect of having to spend three hours on the phone to the not-very-helpful service provider helpline. However, with the family router flashing more than a kids' disco, Dad takes a deep breath and starts speaking to Paula at Plusnet. Three hours later, he turns the power supply off, waits five seconds, turns it back on and the WiFi whips into action. With his pride somewhat dented, Dad informs his delighted teenage offspring that his technical know-how has saved the day again. The WiFi war has been won.

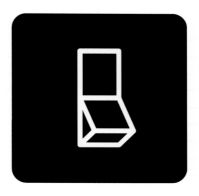

WiFi tip

- Don't do yourself an injury by scrambling behind the TV or the entertainment unit, just to get a glimpse of the WiFi passcode written on the router. Write the code on big pieces of paper and Blu Tak them to the wall of every room in the house.

*XyGG56£+tTjUuU4}>.
Why can't you
remember it?!*

#dothedrivinglessons

At 17, your 'child' is still not able to drink, vote, place a bet or get a mortgage. So while this means they won't be getting drunk at their own housewarming party and putting a tenner on the Conservatives winning a landslide, they could get behind the wheel of Dad's Honda and cruise down the high street. Is that a scarier thought than having Boris Johnson as PM?

Giving driving lessons is one piece of Dadmin that can't be delegated. While you can pay to have your car cleaned and fixed, you can't get someone else to teach your kid how to reverse park. Well, you can, but not at £26 a lesson you won't be. So, Dad and his daughter or son rock up in Morrisons car park at 8am on a Sunday, and tentatively swap seats.

CHECKLIST

 Do... lobby your MP to have the legal driving age raised to, say, 28?

 Don't... play Chris Rea's Road To Hell on the car stereo if you give a driving lesson.

The only advice that Dad actually gives, and that he remembers from his learning days, is the 'mirror, signal, manoeuvre' mantra. With this useless information duly dispatched and after having an intense conversation about the clutch's biting point, your teenager nervously puts the pedal to the metal. And stalls the engine. Then stalls it again, and again.

At the 23rd time of stalling, and with Morrisons about to open at 10am, most Dads will lose patience and begin scrolling through their phones looking for local driving instructors. Yes, £26 does sound like a lot of money, but a new clutch and loss of his no claims discount will be much more costly.

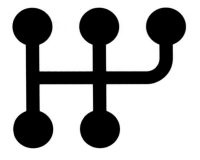

Top tip

- Let Mum give the driving lessons. She has much more patience than you and it's better all round for the wellbeing and harmony of the family. Plus, Dad will get a Sunday morning lie-in.

Remote Dadmin

The Dadmin Journey continues.

Remote Dadmin requires some distance between Dad and his grown-up children. Perhaps they've left for uni or moved out, but despite this, he can never be fully relinquished of his fatherly callings.
He needs proper distance for that to happen, like his kid living at the South Pole and having no access to the internet.

#transferthemoney

Children may fly from your nest, but they'll regularly contact home and ask for a handout. This is where internet banking is a real pain in the wallet for Dad, because no matter what time of day it is, he can always transfer money from his account into his cash-strapped kid's. None of those 'the bank's closed on Wednesday afternoon' or 'the cheque won't clear for five working days' excuses will wash now.

From one perspective, some parents are so keen to pack their child off to university 300 miles away and see their own lives return, that having to make semi-regular money transfers to them is probably a small price to pay. But if you do want to see their face at the family Christmas dinner table, you're gonna need to dish out the extortionate train fare for them before you can dish out the Brussels sprouts.

Remember, university only lasts for three or four years and then this computer cash cow will come to an end. Or maybe not, as then they'll want you to help them buy a car, a big TV and a house.

CHECKLIST

☑ *Do... consider moving to the South Pole and having no access to the internet.*

☒ *Don't... forget to remind the kids that when you're old, you'll expect them to pay for a nice retirement home in return.*

Chart showing parents' disposable income after children.

#dothediy

Dad used to only have to think about the DIY needs at his own place of residence. This could feature Dadmin jobs like weather-proofing the fence, screwing that hinge back on and repairing the light in the cupboard under the stairs, as it's darker and scarier than a cemetery at Halloween in there. But as a father to 'adult kids' who've left home, he now faces the prospect of being on call in case there's a DIY emergency at his son or daughter's place. Without ever agreeing to it, he's become a plumber/builder/engineer on 24-hour standby, ready to respond to desperate phone calls round the clock (with no time off on Sundays or Bank Holidays).

CHECKLIST

 Do... seriously consider charging per hour for your DIY skills.

 Don't... bring a flask of coffee with you. That's taking things too far.

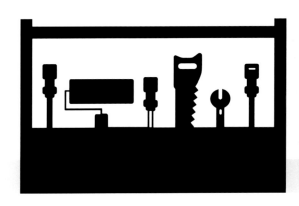

Because of this second job that Dad's reluctantly taken on, his toolbox needs to be in top condition and easily accessible at all times. He must be able to chuck it in the car quickly and speed to his stricken offspring's house, armed with wrenches, pliers and screwdrivers. Of course, whatever tool he needs for the emergency DIY he won't have with him.

This means a journey back to his garage, a rummage for the required equipment and then a trip back to tackle the task. After fixing the dodgy tumble dryer, burst pipe or whatever else he's called upon to sort, Dad will glance at his watch to see it's 3pm and his own plans for the day now lie in ruins. This is when DIY Emergency Dad becomes Grumpy Dad, especially as his son or daughter have not even offered him a cup of coffee and a biscuit in all the time he's been there. It seems like Do It Yourself refers to everything at this house.

Any chance of a coffee?

Top tip

- Don't make a better job of the DIY at your children's homes than you do at your own place. Your partner will question your home DIY skills, which will upset you.

#havetoolsready

Following on from remote Dadmin DIY emergencies is the business of tools. Specifically, the lending out of your tools to your children so that they can think about doing their own odd jobs and DIY in their own home.

There's no point in hiding your tools away in the shed. As you discovered on page 80, your daughter or son already know that the shed padlock key is not-very-secretly stashed under the plant pot, so that trick's foiled. Sometimes Dad will have been made aware that his tools and gadgets have been 'borrowed', usually via a text asking if they can be taken, followed by another message four minutes later declaring that they have indeed been taken.

CHECKLIST

☑ Do... take a picture of your son/daughter holding your tool that they've borrowed. You'll then have a digital record and receipt.

☒ Don't... demand to have 'Harry the Hacksaw' back. Never tell anyone that you name your tools.

If common or garden screwdrivers, hammers, tile cutters and handsaws go missing, that's not too bad to accept. But, if Dad's new DeWalt Double Bevel Sliding Compound Mitre Saw and Karcher Premium Window Vac suddenly go walkies, then he's likely to go on the warpath. Not that he's ever intending to use a mitre saw or window vac, but he likes to know that he could, one day, if he gets the urge.

So once Dad visits his child's house to check up on his tools, he falls into the trap of ending up using them to carry out the DIY job there. In fact, his tools are only really ever used to sort other people's DIY problems, leaving his own list of Dadmin repairs and fixes at home to grow ever longer. Just like the grass, because you've lent out the lawnmower.

DIY (and random) things Dads lend their kids...

- lawnmower
- stepladder
- ladder
- paintbrushes
- workbench
- car
- cash card
- PIN code

Steve

#sortthecar

'Sorting' your son or daughter's car is different to fixing, cleaning, taxing and insuring it. Well, only in the way that it's a little bit of all of these things, which means it's exactly the same as fixing, cleaning, taxing and insuring their car. That was a waste of two sentences, wasn't it? Now make that four sentences. Doh!

Even though they are no longer resident at your house 24/7, Dad will still find himself being a remote vehicle looker-after person. 'Sorting' starts with helping your child to buy their car. They want it to have a top-notch stereo, climate control and comfy leather seats. You want it to be cheap, safe and practical. They want it to have black alloys and a panoramic sunroof. You want it to be cheap to run and have such a small engine that an eggcup of petrol will get it to Inverness and back again.

CHECKLIST

 Do... ask your child to clean their car at least once a year. Being able to see out of the windscreen is a good thing.

 Don't... offer to take it for its MOT, as you'll be forced to 'offer' to pay for that too.

Between you both, you compromise on something like a Toyota Aygo or a Peugeot 108. You take great delight in telling them that, in fact, these two motors share 70 per cent of their components and are actually built in the same factory. Their face is somewhat less delighted upon hearing this irrelevant news.

After the purchase, taxing and insuring has been dealt with, your child can hit the open road and enjoy the freedom of motoring. Not that enjoyment was a criteria you paid much attention to when sorting out this car, as the little Aygo or 108 barely has enough room inside to change gear without the driver's elbow breaking the passenger's ribs. And there's definitely not enough room to pack luggage for a trip to Inverness.

Grand Dadmin

Nice one, old boy!

It's the final phase of Dadmin. To reach the legendary level of Grand Dadmin duties, you've passed through the earlier periods of fatherly tasks and just when you think it's time to put your feet up, your grandfather jobs take hold. So grab a biscuit, grab the pushchair and get going, Grandad!

#makeacuppa

1. Fill the kettle, but only to the required level for the number of cups of tea being consumed. You're pretty sure electricity doesn't grow on trees.

2. Grab a teabag. Your favourite brand of teabag obviously, because at this stage of your life you know what you like.

3. Gently drop the teabag in the mug.

4. Watch the kettle boil (it's a rather relaxing thing).

5. Think back to a time when kettles whistled, to when you used to whistle and seemingly the whole world whistled.

6. Pour the newly-boiled water in the mug. It must be newly boiled, as just 'hot' water doesn't make such a top brew.

7. Stir the teabag (slowly).

8. Squash the teabag (slowly) on the inside of the mug.

9. Take the semi-dried teabag to the bin, being careful not to drip on the floor and make another Grand Dadmin cleaning job.

10. Pour the milk in until the tea's the right shade of golden brown.

11. Drink the tea.

12. Make that soothing 'aah' sound after the first sip.

#babysitting

Grandads, don't be fooled. Although it's called babysitting, what it should be named is 'looking after someone who may no longer be a baby but is still technically your grandchild'. Babysitting Dadmin can begin at just a few weeks into the child's life, and last well into their teenage years.

Don't fret though, because it does get easier with time. When your grandkids are babies and kids, the babysitting duties cover nappy changing, feeding, bathing, playing with toys and constantly watching Mr Tumble on iPlayer. By the time they reach about eight years old, babysitting really just means having to be in the same house as the child because they can pretty much look after themselves. They can certainly operate iPlayer at that stage with no adult help needed. Easy peasy.

Grandads, just make sure you have an end time – and date – arranged for collection of the kids. If the children are dropped with you at, say, 6pm on Friday, don't let your son or daughter disappear with an "I'll collect them later" ringing in your ears. "Later" could mean 9pm that night, 2pm tomorrow or next Thursday.

CHECKLIST

 Do... be prepared to be woken at 5.32am if the grandkids are sleeping over.

 Don't... expect the grandkids to sit quietly and watch Antiques Roadshow with you.

#pushthepushchairagain

Remember when you pushed your own kids in prams and buggies? It's a good job you have that experience to call upon, because part of your Grand Dadmin duties will be to do it all again and cart your grandchild down the street and through parks in a big lump of collapsible plastic, metal and wheels. Such fun.

Pushing is the easy part, though. The difficult bit is familiarising yourself with precisely how the pushchair functions. You'll be asking yourself things like, 'How do the brakes work? What's this lever for? Does this button operate the instant baby-quieting mode?' Collapsing and then un-re-collapsing the pushchair is very tricky and could require days reading the instruction manual. But the most annoying part will be when you discover it won't fit in your car boot while your golf clubs are also in there. Take a big sigh, because you'll be seeing more of the local soft play centre than you will of greens and fairways.

CHECKLIST

 Do... keep several packets of raisins in the pushchair pocket. You'll need the energy for all that pushing.

 Don't... just dust off and use that old pushchair in your loft from 27 years ago.

#tellthestoriesagain

Tell The Stories can be two things in Grand Dadmin. Firstly, Grandfathers will be called upon to read lots of bedtime stories together with a grandchild. He'll notice that the themes and basic narrative structure in the books are the same as when he read to his own children back in the day. But, people's names will have changed from Kevin, Gareth and Michelle to modern names like Poppy, Grace, Noah and Oscar. And these bedtime story characters won't interact in the park or playground like they used to 20 or 30 years ago. Now, Poppy and her posse meet up at WiFi hotspots, outdoor activity centres and gluten free cafes.

The other aspect to Tell The Stories is talking about the old days with your grandchildren. They'll love hearing all about cars that had windows that went up and down by turning a handle, or that drinking water came from the tap and not the fridge or a bottle. In fact, such entertaining tales will send them to sleep quicker than any bedtime fiction will.

CHECKLIST

 Do... use voices and sound effects when reading stories (see page 29).

 Don't... tell that tale of you finding two dead frogs in the shed. That's a horror story for a four year old.

#spoilthegrandkids

In the dictionary, 'spoil' means 'to give someone anything and everything they want'. Grandads are quite partial to the odd bit of grandkid spoiling. This could extend to buying an ice cream, dishing out cookies, getting that Lego set and letting the kids stay up past their bedtime. It could also mean upgrading the Xbox 360 to a Xbox One X 1TB 4K, but fortunately ice lollies are far cheaper and easier to operate.

There's nothing wrong with spoiling the grandkids. It's one of the most rewarding and simplest aspects of Grand Dadmin. It makes the child feel special, it makes you feel special and it shows how much you love indulging and putting a smile on the face of the little ones. Just remember that the dictionary also describes spoiling as 'destroying something or making it less valuable'. That could happen to your house if, on a hot day, you tell your grandchild there are no ice lollies left in your freezer.

#fixeverythingagain

By the time you reach being a Grandad, do you honestly think all the fixing and repairing of stuff will be done? Surely there's nothing left to mend, service, correct or improve by now? Wrong.

There's plenty of fixing to be done in the years ahead. In all the time you've occupied this planet, you've acquired many personal things that still require your attention. And now that you're a Grandad, your Grand Dadmin includes patching up and repairing bits and pieces that belong to, or are connected to, your grandkids. From the outside these won't appear to be complex tasks or items – much simpler than fixing the lawnmower, say. But once you set about trying to fathom why a radio controlled helicopter won't fly, or how to untie the laces from PE trainers, you'll soon realise fixing everything when a Grandad is a full-time job. It's a vacancy that you wouldn't apply for in a hurry, either.

CHECKLIST

 Do... fake smile as you pretend to enjoy fixing everything again.

 Don't... bury your screwdrivers in the garden as a way to get out of it.

Top Grand Dadmin items to fix

1. Scooter
2. Bike
3. Nerf blaster
4. New scooter
5. Bedside light
6. Trampoline
7. Toys (miscellaneous)
8. That other scooter

#putmyfeetup

At some point in Grand Dadmin, putting your feet up will be possible (usually when Countdown is on).

Can you solve this conundrum?

| C | D | E | K | R | A | N | K | E |

Dadmin's not all about serious stuff like looking after kids, cars and houses. It's about having a laugh too! Prepare for these classic Dad jokes...

Why do Dads love scarecrows?
Because they're outstanding in their fields.

How many Dads does it take to change a light bulb?
What was the light doing on in the first place?

Why did the Dad get a job collecting leaves?
Because he was raking it in.

Why couldn't the Dad stand his kid's bike up?
It was two tyred.

What did the Dad say to the zero?
Thanks for nothing.

Why did the Dad stop buying Velcro?
Because it was a rip off.

Why did the Dad give cough medicine to the pony?
It was a little horse.

What does the Daddy buffalo say to his
lad every morning when he leaves for work?
Bison.

If a Dad has no body and no nose, what's he called?
Nobody knows.

Why did the Dad cry when his daughter cut her wedding cake?
Because it was in tiers.

What award do Dads get for telling knock-knock jokes?
The no-bell prize.

Dad, did you get a haircut?
No, I got them all cut.

LEARN THE LANGUAGE
PHRASES
LEARN THE MEANINGS

Dads, are you stuck for what to say when faced with Dadmin? Or perhaps you're someone trying to translate what a Dadmin word or saying actually means? Luckily, the Dadmin phrasebook and dictionary is at hand!

"What are we doing this weekend, honey?"
Translation: *"I hope I'm not cleaning the car, tidying the garage, walking the dog, building a wardrobe and going in the loft all weekend, honey?"*

What time do we have to leave?"
Translation: *"What's the latest time I have to stop doing something I enjoy, like sitting on the sofa, in order to do something I don't enjoy, like visiting your auntie?"*

"I think I'll cut the grass."
Translation: *"I'll think about cutting the grass for three hours, then I'll move to actually begin cutting the grass, then it'll rain."*

"Whose turn is it to empty the dishwasher?"
Translation: *"It's not my turn."*

"Now, I'll just give it a gentle tap with my hammer…"
Translation: *"I'm gonna smash this thing up."*

"What's that you're watching on TV?"
Translation: *"Turn it over now."*

"YES!"
Translation: *"I'm answering your question in the affirmative, but in an ever-so-slightly angry tone."*

"It'll only take me five minutes."
Translation: *"This Dadmin job will take a minimum of five minutes and a maximum of five days, depending on how bored I get."*

"Where's my crowbar?"
Translation: *"I've broken my hammer, so I'll smash this thing up with that instead."*

"Er, can you get mum here please, kids?"
Translation: *"Er, I've messed this up and now I'm in trouble."*

"Yeeeeeeessss!"
Translation: *"I'm very happy that this rather tedious Dadmin has been dealt with successfully."*

"Now?"
Translation: *"Do you really want me to do that thing this instant, when I'm perfectly happy not having to do it?"*

#dadmindone

So much Dadmin to do...

 Kids cleaned, fed, teeth and hair brushed

 Spiders caught

 Holes drilled

 Screws screwed

 Fence fixed

 Dinner cooked

 Car cleaned

So much Dadmin to do...

- Homework done
- WiFi working
- Rubbish taken out
- Lunch box packed
- Batteries charged
- Pocket money paid
- Shopping put away
- Washing-up sorted

Relax – the Dadmin is done... until tomorrow.

#index ☝

DADMIN DOES NOT COME WITH AN INDEX!
DOES LIFE COME WITH AN INDEX? NO, SIR.

THE ONLY THINGS THAT COME WITH AN INDEX ARE THE
SCREWFIX AND ARGOS CATALOGUES. ADMITTEDLY, THESE
ARE VERY HELPFUL WHEN YOU NEED TO QUICKLY FIND A
700 WATT GENERATOR OR A LEGO FRIENDS SET. HMM.
MAYBE THIS DADMIN BOOK SHOULD HAVE AN INDEX?
SADLY, AFTER BANGING ON ABOUT GENERATORS AND
LEGO, THERE'S NO ROOM FOR IT NOW. SORRY.